# Write Right!

## Writing

# BOOK REPORTS

By Benjamin Proudfit

**Gareth Stevens**
PUBLISHING

Please visit our website, www.garethstevens.com. For a free color catalog of all our high-quality books, call toll free 1-800-542-2595 or fax 1-877-542-2596.

**Library of Congress Cataloging-in-Publication Data**

Proudfit, Benjamin.
Writing book reports / by Benjamin Proudfit.
p. cm. — (Write right!)
Includes index.
ISBN 978-1-4824-0805-8 (pbk.)
ISBN 978-1-4824-1513-1 (6-pack)
ISBN 978-1-4824-0804-1 (library binding)
1. Report writing — Juvenile literature. 2. Book reviewing — Juvenile literature. I. Title.
LB1047.3 P76 2015
372.13028—d23

First Edition

Published in 2015 by
**Gareth Stevens Publishing**
111 East 14th Street, Suite 349
New York, NY 10003

Copyright © 2015 Gareth Stevens Publishing

Designer: Sarah Liddell
Editor: Kristen Rajczak

Photo credits: Cover, p. 1 Monkey Business Images/Shutterstock.com; pp. 5, 17 luminaimages/Shutterstock.com; p. 7 Pressmaster/Shutterstock.com; p. 9 MJTH/Shutterstock.com; p. 11 iofoto/Shutterstock.com; p. 13 Vietrov Dmytro/Shutterstock.com; p. 15 sirastock/Shutterstock.com; p. 19 Valery Sidelnykov/Shutterstock.com; p. 21 (background) mexrix/Shutterstock.com; p. 21 (boy) Gelpi JM/Shutterstock.com.

Printed in the United States of America

CPSIA compliance information: Batch #CS15GS: For further information contact Gareth Stevens, New York, New York at 1-800-542-2595.

# CONTENTS

All About Book Reports . . . . . . . . . . 4

Choosing the Book . . . . . . . . . . . . 6

Read, Read, Read . . . . . . . . . . . . 8

Follow Directions!. . . . . . . . . . . . 10

The Summary . . . . . . . . . . . . . . 12

Who's It About? . . . . . . . . . . . . 14

Stating Your Opinion . . . . . . . . . . 16

Other Sections . . . . . . . . . . . . . 18

Revising . . . . . . . . . . . . . . . . . 20

Glossary. . . . . . . . . . . . . . . . . 22

For More Information. . . . . . . . . . 23

Index . . . . . . . . . . . . . . . . . . 24

Words in the glossary appear in **bold** type the first time they are used in the text.

# ALL ABOUT BOOK REPORTS

Reading helps you learn more words and understand what other people's lives are like, and can take you to places you've never been. Writing a book report gives you a chance to practice giving your thoughts about a piece of writing. This is a useful skill as you'll have to do this throughout your school years and after.

Writing a book report begins when you get your **assignment**. It will let you know how long you have to get the report done.

## ON THE WRITE TRACK

Book reports may be written about nonfiction books, or those based on real-life events. This book will focus mostly on **fiction**, though the suggestions offered can be easily applied to book reports on nonfiction.

You must know when your book report needs to be turned in. That will help you plan when to start reading your book!

BOOK REPORT DUE

5

# CHOOSING THE BOOK

If you get to choose the book you write a report on, the first step is to pick that book! You should choose one you'll enjoy. So, if you like history, choose something that takes place in the past. Animal lovers should choose something with animal characters, like *Charlotte's Web* by E. B. White.

Your teacher may give you a list of books to choose from. Look each one up at the library or online to see which one is most interesting to you.

## ON THE WRITE TRACK

Sometimes you'll be assigned the book to report on, or you won't like your choices. That's okay! Giving books you might not normally pick a chance can help you find or learn something new.

Still aren't sure what to choose? Ask your classmates or teacher for ideas. They might have read something they think you'll like.

# READ, READ, READ

The most important part of writing a good book report is reading the book you're writing about! Make sure you give yourself enough time to finish the whole thing.

Keep some paper and a pencil with you while you're reading. Write down any big story changes, what you think of the characters, and anything else that grabs your attention. Taking these notes will help you remember the book better later. You can use them when you start to write your report.

## ON THE WRITE TRACK

Learning about a book's author can improve your understanding of the book. Where authors are from and events from their life often play a part in the books they write.

Sometimes teachers will give you a sheet to fill out while you're reading. On it, you might list major characters, the **setting**, and other **details**. This or your own notes will act as an outline for your report.

# FOLLOW DIRECTIONS!

Now that you've gathered your notes, it's time to read over your assignment again. What **specific** instructions has your teacher given?

It's common for teachers to want a book report done in a certain way. Your assignment may tell you to use a computer to type and print your report. Some teachers will ask you to use lined paper and your best handwriting. Be sure to include your name and class or grade on it!

## ON THE WRITE TRACK

When you're asked to type a book report, your teacher may tell you what **font** size to use and how the report should be spaced on the page.

The title and author of the book you read should be included at the beginning of your report.

# THE SUMMARY

Book reports are commonly divided into sections. Some teachers will ask you to list the title of each new section at its beginning. Others will want the report simply broken up into **paragraphs**. Always follow the directions you've been given.

The summary is a short retelling of the story you read. It doesn't need to include a lot of detail, but should sum up the **plot**. The summary section of your book report should include the book's **tone** and setting.

## ON THE WRITE TRACK

Using transition words such as "in the beginning," "then," and "after" will help you keep your summary in time order.

Pay close attention to length when writing a summary. It's easy to get carried away recounting the story! If a word or page count isn't included in your assignment, ask your teacher how long the summary should be.

# WHO'S IT ABOUT?

The main characters in your book should be easy to pick out. They're the ones the story is about!

When writing about a character, think about how you would introduce that character to a friend. You would use **adjectives** like "brave" or "smart" and tell why you think that word applies to them. Read the example below about Wilbur from *Charlotte's Web*.

Wilbur the pig is loyal and kind. He always helps his friends, such as when he guards Charlotte's babies after she dies.

## ON THE WRITE TRACK

Be sure to "show" a character's personality—don't just tell about it. In the example, you'll see that a specific detail from the story is used to show Wilbur's loyalty and kindness.

Depending on the book you read, your section on characters may have just one entry or many! Make sure to note if one of the characters is the **narrator**.

# Characters

Wilbur

Charlotte

Fern

Templeton

Mr. Zuckerman

# STATING YOUR OPINION

As you're reading, write down what you think about your book. Use these notes for the opinion part of your book report.

First, clearly state what you thought of the book. Then, show why you felt that way. Look at this example:

I liked *Matilda* by Roald Dahl. It's fun to read about a kid who is smarter than the adults around her! The author included great details so I could easily imagine the story happening, like when Matilda puts glue on her father's hat.

## ON THE WRITE TRACK

You may be asked to include whether or not you would **recommend** this book, and to whom, in your opinion section. Make sure you give clear reasons for your statement.

If you didn't like the book you read, say so! But remember to also write why you didn't like it.

# OTHER SECTIONS

There are many other sections that could be included in a book report. One could be about the main idea of the book, or what the book is about overall. This is different from the summary. It's just one or two sentences. One main idea of *Matilda* might be that our differences are what make us special.

Favorite quotes, or lines from the book, may be another part. Keep an eye out for quotes you like as you read if your assignment includes this section.

## ON THE WRITE TRACK

When you write a quote from a book, use quotation marks around the line. This one is from *Charlotte's Web*: "When I say 'salutations,' it's just my fancy way of saying hello or good morning."

The main idea might not seem clear to you at first. Think about how you would describe the book to someone if you only had one sentence to do so. That can help!

19

# REVISING

After you've finished writing the sections of your book report, it's time to revise, or make changes. Read it over. Does it all make sense? Make sure you haven't left out part of the plot. Check each sentence carefully to make sure it has a capital letter, subject, verb, and punctuation at the end, such as a period or exclamation point.

Make any changes you need to before you turn in your finished book report. Double-check that you've put your name on it!

## ON THE WRITE TRACK

The subject is what a sentence is about. The verb is the action the subject is doing. You need both for a sentence to be complete!

# TIPS FOR WRITING A BOOK REPORT SUMMARY

Answer the following questions, and you'll have a well-written, brief summary section.

- → Where and when does the story take place?

- → Whom is the story about?

- → What major problems do the characters face?

- → How do they solve these problems?

- → In what ways do the characters change as a result?

- → How does the story end?

# GLOSSARY

**adjective:** a word that says something about a person, place, or thing

**assignment:** a task or amount of work given to do

**detail:** a small part

**fiction:** a made-up story

**font:** a style of lettering

**narrator:** the person who tells a story. It may be one of the story's characters.

**paragraph:** a group of sentences having to do with one idea or topic

**plot:** the main story of a book

**recommend:** make a suggestion

**setting:** where and when a story takes place

**specific:** clearly stated

**tone:** the general feeling of a piece of writing

# FOR MORE INFORMATION

## BOOKS

Collins, Terry. *Whatever Says Mark: Knowing and Using Punctuation.* North Mankato, MN: Picture Window Books, 2014.

Fogarty, Mignon. *Grammar Girl Presents the Ultimate Writing Guide for Students.* New York, NY: Henry Holt and Company, 2011.

Minden, Cecilia, and Kate Roth. *How to Write a Book Report.* Ann Arbor, MI: Cherry Lake Publishing, 2011.

## WEBSITES

### How to Write a Book Report
*kids.usa.gov/articles/book-report/index.shtml*
Answering the questions on this website will help guide you through many of the topics needed in your book report.

### The Reading Nook
*www.thereadingnook.com/third_grade*
Do you get to choose your own book? Get some ideas of good book-report books here!

# INDEX

assignment  4, 10, 13, 18

author  8, 11

characters  9, 14, 15, 21

choose book  6, 7

details  9, 12, 14, 16

fiction  4

main idea  18, 19

nonfiction  4

notes  8, 9, 10, 16

opinion  16

outline  9

paragraphs  12

plot  12, 20

quotes  18

revise  20

sections  12, 15, 16, 18, 20

setting  9, 12

summary  12, 13, 18, 21

transition words  12